It's not the pen,
the aesthetically unpleasing desk you sit upon,
It's not about the time of day or the moonlight that
has gone away, or the starlight that seemed so shy,
or the way the butterfly flapped it's wings as you
saw it fly. It's not the pale skin or the wrinkled
lines, or the extra lumps and bumps sitting
beneath your clothes that you hide at all times, it's
not the way the notebook feels or the size of your
heels or the colour of your hair or the freckles that
sit upon your face, just like the ones before you,
the generational split. It's just about you, and you
being you and all that you are and all that you do.
It's about you being you with the freckle face, there
is no competition, and no real race.
Only you against you in this stint that is life. And
we get to choose, if we win or lose, as we hold the
power and all of the keys, and if your asking me, I'll
tell you the truth - that it's always been you, you
see that now right? That it was just wasted to be so
uptight, and it was not worth having the fight, the
one in the mirror when you wanted to see, a
different you looking back, it was me.
It was just me, it was all me,
The wind in my hair and in my sails,
Pushing you forward and shouting loud wails,
Words of self love, of true self compassion, or
cheering you on when you had nothing left, when
you felt heartbroken, lost and bereft.
It was all you,
It was all true,
And all that it is,

And all that is new,
All that's to come from these whispered hours, of
knights with there swords climbing the towers,
And stories of castles and blackberry bushes, and
poetry written beneath all the shushes, and times
of too much, or being a lot, times you remember
and ones you forgot. None of this matters. It's all
just in dreams, and non of it really is all as seems.
So let down your hair and raise up the draw,
because nobody really has done this before.

I am a poet, as free as a bird.

My soul sings the words that need to be heard.

With fire in my belly and a pen in my hand, I write words of life that expand through the land.

I am a poet, with tales of love.

My heart feels emotions that fly like a dove. They accept and let go, soaring high up above.

I am a poet, with moments of grief.

The pain that fuels life, testing faith and belief.

I am a poet, as free as a bird. I hold inside, the poems that need to be heard.

The Power of Words

Do you understand the power of your words?
Surely I hope you do.

Take a look at the lady you just complemented on
her outfit - did you see her change of confidence -
yes, that came from you!

Do you understand the power of your words? I
really think you should.

That cutting snipe in anger, it caused pain - and
from that came no good.

Do you understand the power of your words -
when you speak out to the universe or angels
flying high?

They listen to your prayers and calls, they listen as
you speak. They watch you through this life - and
oh my goodness they do try.

They try to tell you everyday about the power of
your words.

How you can make a strangers day, or be that
sunshine in the grey.

How you can crush a persons hope with words of
discouragement and anger.

You see words are pretty powerful and do not wash away with soap.

Do you understand the power of your words, I truly hope you do.

For these words we speak to ourselves and others, these words just may come true.

Ideal world

We say 'in an ideal world', but what does that really mean?

What's more ideal than sunsets, rainbows or fields of green?

The laughter of children, the flutter of love, what is this ideal world we speak of flying high like a dove.

What's more ideal than the wind on your face? Or the beautiful softness when speaking with grace.

We say in an ideal world, but what does that mean? Could it be this world that we have unseen.

Unseen all the beauty this world has to offer, unseen all the love this world has to give - Open your eyes to the life that you have yet to live!

If you wait for this world you speak of so much, you may miss all the love you can feel through a touch.

If you wait for this world you speak of so often, you may miss the way our human hearts soften.

Soften at beauty and soften with love, don't wait for that world, look within and above.

'You are allowed to be both a masterpiece and a work in progress'
Sophie Blush

Raise a Glass

Why do we raise a glass?
Why do we always say cheers?
Why has this poison become the go too, for so
many, so many years.

Why is it there when we stress?
Why is it there when we smile?
Could it be we've lost our way, for just a little
while.

I feel new winds amongst us,
The feeling of change is around.
A new way of thinking fills the air,
Fresh pastures to be found.

There is life to be lived and memories made.
Ones that deserve to be felt,
not regrets to be replayed.

Possibilities endless with clarity given. Your story
is waiting, yet to be written.

So why do we raise a glass?
Why do we always say cheers?
Let's change that tradition I say,
Let's be the pioneers.

Raised Right

They say they should be quiet, well mannered and must not make a fuss.

To be seen and not heard people say, I heard it when they raised us.

They say uniform does good, and in some ways I agree. But does it leave room for expression or creation - or does it imprint thoughts of 'you should'

You should tow the line, you must get a job, have a family, pay taxes and don't have free time!

Free time to be happy, free time to relax. Free time to play, create, laugh and run.

As we raise our children in this fast changing world, I'll do it with mixtures of love, wisdom - in a pot all as one swirl.

Wisdom of kindness, love of strength, words of warmth, and tales of freedom.

I'll raise them to be so much better than me, they will say what they want and conform when they feel. Feel it is right and just to do so, not when it's from a voice of 'because I said so'

Question authority, ask for there reasons. Make sure life's fair, and do this all seasons.

So they say 'raise them right' oh I will, you will see. I'll raise them with courage of love and the strength to be free.

Our path is our path and ours alone

We don't have a guide book, and can't wait around
to be shown.

To compare your journey with others is futile,
Our dirt underfoot is different,
Our rocks and fallen debris not the same.

Don't follow another into the woods, that pathway
is not yours.

Do not look and see others ahead, or berate your
self for taking a rest, changing direction does not
mean a fail, for this is your path, your very own
trail.

The path you create is filled with your essence, the
flowers you've grown are all your creation.

Yours looks different from mine, and isn't that
beautiful.

We can look onto others for sense of direction, ask
for advice and value connection. Lend a lamp from
a friend in the darkness, for after all, you are
human.

But walk your own path, live your truth. Fly your
own banner and grow your own flowers. Move the
debris and swing from the trees, have an

adventure and make it your own, don't look onto others or wait to be shown.

Our path is our path and ours alone, and it's a beautiful pathway of all that is true, all that's been dealt with, all that's to come, and above all else, It's all that is you.

Connection

I thrive from connection, it gives me direction. It's the fuel to my fire and breaths air to my lungs.

I have a life of experience, and a soul filled with wisdom.
From growing, learning and losing direction.

If we learn from each other and share our experience.

If my pain helps your pain then life's not in vain, by keeping connection there's so much to gain.

So let's stick together and talk it all out,
our worries and stresses, you might even shout.

If we shut out connection, we loose our direction,
we'll look back one day and regret on reflection.

I'm here for you, you're here for me, the connection is real, it helps calm our sea.

Bring back all the colour

We thought it would be boring,
Dull and lonely it must be ,
We thought that we'd have nothing left, bleakness
far to see.

Conditioned to believe, what's life without the
wine?! Raised up side by side, it's what we turn to
every time.

The lies it told to you, the lies it told to me, and for
the first time in our lives, now we finally see.

Freedom doesn't live in the bottom of a glass, it
doesn't live in there at all, it drowns us by the
mass.

One day at a time, one foot in front of the other.
Step by step we make our way, and bring back all
the colour.

The colour we had lost, enthusiasm waned, it will
all come back I promise, a thawing of the frost.

Sober life's not boring, it's not all rainbows either,
but give yourself a chance, and take a little
breather.

First Click

It's all on that first click, something just makes sense. After years and years of trying, and sitting on the fence.

You realise it's poison, you realise it's lies, all just one illusion, built up over time.

'Education' and your 'why' - that's what you need to find. Look inside to find these, look deep within your mind.

Every failed attempt, was not a fail at all, every time you slipped up, you got up from the fall.

The days they build and build, then one day you just find, the sober life you wanted, you got it as you willed.

I won't shrink for you

I won't shrink for you, or silence my noise. I'll raise
up my voice and shout it out loud!

I won't be small to fit, or follow the crowd. I'll grow
and expand and cover more ground.

If my voice makes you shudder and my words
make you cross, then just leave me be - it's really
no loss!

I'll raise my voice, I'll shout loud, I'll grow and
expand,
And the ones who don't like it,
fall away just like sand.

Mummy Wine

There's this thing called mummy wine, became a culture over time,
Made us all feel 'normal',
Like excessive drinking was just fine!

'Kids acting like a dick, pour a large one quick!'

'It's fine to have one more, look at the mess down on the floor!'

But here's the thing, it wasn't fine. It encouraged me to lean on wine,
I wasn't dealing with the mess,
the tantrums felt so loud,
I wasn't coping well at all and all it did was cause more clouds.

You see I don't need wine or gin to deal with my kids, I never needed that at all,

What I needed was a clear head, not to follow, only to be so misled.

What I needed was advice, a friend to lend a hand. What I needed was group of mums that said, 'we understand'.

We thought it was just normal, to grab that other bottle, look around - YOU are normal, that's what they said, that was our 'model'.

So now I'm calling time on all that 'mummy wine',
And I really think it's bullshit, if you just think 'it's
fine'!

See through

Let's be see through,
Let's let the world see,
All that I am, and all that is me

If you can see through me,
Then maybe you'll see,
All that your going through,
You soon will be free

If I show you my pain,
If I open up,
Maybe it helps you,
With filling your cup

Let's take of the masks, the painted on smiles,
Let's walk together,
Let's go for miles

We share and we talk,
We lighten the load,
We keep on going,
Side by side down the road.

100 days

I didn't think I'd get here! Not ever never ever!

A year ago a 5 day challenge seemed so hard,
I cried, I'd failed, I'd never do it - succumbed to life
as it was then.

I dusted myself of, I stood back on my feet, I tried
and tried again, building days up over time, and
never losing sight.

I could see the life I wanted, the life I knew I
deserved. It may of not been easy, but I now thank
every challenge.

Every challenge made me stronger, I grew and
grew and grew. I read the books and joined the
groups. I listened to the podcasts, over and over
again.

Connection was my key, it truly set me free. In
sharing and listening the click, it happened, it had
finally happened for me.

I'm so glad I never gave up, I'm glad I kept showing
up. I continued with self care, over filling my own
cup!

I made it, I made it, I got to 100 days! I'll shout this
from the roof tops!
I'm as proud as proud can be!

Magic

The magic is real,
We believed it once! Let's remember, let's believe!

Through the eyes of a child, anything is possible,
nothing unreachable, the sky is the limit!

Twinkling stars, rustling leaves, they all come to
life through the power of imagination,

But the power is you, you make it real, you did that
once, so do it again.

Let's remember, let's believe!

Let's take a walk

Let's take a walk, a walk in the woods, let's do up
our coats and pull up our hoods

Let's stomp our feet in crunchy brown leaves, and
let's tell tall tales of goodies and thieves.

Let's breathe in the air of the warm winter sun,
and let's forget troubles, not go home til' we're
done.

Listen to sounds of nothing but silence, let's look to
the trees and ask them for guidance

Letting it go, and letting it be, being in nature, it
helps, come and see...

Let's take a walk, a walk in the woods

To my younger self

A letter to my younger self, oh my, what would I
say,

I'd start of with some self belief, an
anchor come what may.

Believe in yourself, and keep on believing, you are
your biggest supporter,

That girl in the mirror, put her first! She is you, and
she deserves the world,

Don't look for her faults or chase false perfection,
dance through the mistakes and lose your
direction,

Follow your dreams and never give up, build your
resilience and keep moving up,

Don't look to others to love and support you, first
look within, it's all in there, you'll see

Cherish and be grateful for the ones that you love,
the ones that love you and love love love, the world
needs more of it,

Never give up, never give in, keep moving, keep
going - you'll get there I promise, only you can win

There's no competition with anyone else, no one to impress, only yourself.

Go grab the world, go find your wings, fly fly fly as high as you can,
Be free as a bird

Go rule the world, my beautiful girl

I Hold

I hold a lot inside,
Lots of stuff inside my head.

I hold onto the past, and things that I regret.

I hold onto the moments, when I have felt like me.

I hold onto the passing thoughts, of how some
things could be.

I hold onto my passions, for the poetry of life.

I hold onto my husbands hand, through good times
and through strife.

I hold a lot inside, things that go unseen, inside my
mind of love and growth - perhaps it looks serene.

Feel the pain

Feel the pain, let it all In.
Tears they should fall, else they build up within.

It all has to flow, so release and let go,
Forgive and step forward, don't drown in the sea of
sorrow.

If we hold onto pain, if we fear the hurt we build
up our walls and pack them with dirt.

Keeping them out, locking you in,
Safe for now but never feeling or growing, staying
stuck in this place with no freedom to shout.

So shout it all out, let it all flow, embrace into the
pain and then watch yourself grow.

Rise

May this be the year I rise,
May this be the year I bloom

All the wisdom and tears,
All of the fights and the fears

All come together as words of advice,
Poems and stories of not thinking twice

May this be my year to shine, with all of my words
in a rhyme,

May I let go of worries and fears, holding me back
for all of these years

May this be the year of me,
The one when I truly just 'be'

The one where I reach for the stars, knowing it
could all be ours

Shall we

Shall we just dance like no one is watching?
Shall we just move to the music and not care to be perfect?
Shall we just allow ourselves the freedom to move, to hear the beat and to shuffle our feet!

Shall we just let loose to a song?
Shall we just dance? Shall we just move? Shall we just feel free and dance all night long?

Shall we just turn up the music? Dance through the days, the good ones the hard ones and all ones in between?

Shall we just dance?

Be nothing but true

Do you remember when you were two? You never cared then who was looking at you.

Do you remember when you were four? You jumped round the world in all your galore.

Do you remember when you were 10? Making up games, it was so simple then.

Now look in the mirror and see that it's you, still in there, still waiting for a chance to shine through.

Let her dance, let her play, let her make some mistakes.
Let her be silly, let her choose, let her eat some more cakes.

Stop worrying yourself with what others think.
Look in that mirror, see that it's you, then go out in the world and be nothing but true.

The Dim Light

There's something very calming, sitting with only dim light,
We sit in the hue, the day has passed, it's nearly night.

Feeling warm, and processing our thoughts, with not much light at all. Feeling our way, with only inner thoughts to lead us.

The bright light would be to much, illuminating to Wildly, I think I'll sit with just the dim light, for a little longer, while I process quietly.

Free

Once you decide to be free,
To pull down the mask and let them all see,

Once you decide to be you,
Not worry for worries and just see it through,

Once you decide to be wild,
Not tamed or silenced, like the mindset of child,

Once you decide to be flawed,
Yet still loved and cherished and always adored,

Once you decide to be, perfectly imperfect for the world to see,

Once you decide all that, well really there's no holding you back,
Because once you decide to be free, you'll be as happy as happy can be.

Dear my previous self,

I see all your attempts, your worries and your
doubts.
I see all of your efforts, your talents and your
beauty.
I see you sitting on the curious fence and
wondering if you should take the leap,
I see the times you regret, and think you won't
move forward, but listen to these words I speak
and hear them in your soul.

You won't be boring, lonely or bored, believe me, it
is true.
You won't lose friends, or have nothing to do, for
you will still be you.

You won't fall down this time, I promise, this time
it's going to last.
What's done is done, regrets don't help, let's leave
them in the past.

The future holds connection, ones that are so true.
The future holds love and friendship, from people
you never knew.

Your days will be so bright, free from all the
thoughts, your evenings seem much longer, and
you use them as you ought.

You'll be the parent you always knew you were, full of patience, love and strength. Believe me they are watching, and they do follow in your steps.

Your life may not be perfect, but soon it will be close. By removing that old crutch, you'll get the things you want the most.

Not enough

You're not enough,
You never will be.

You are not perfect, or flawless.

Your house isn't gleaming with out a speck of dust
to be seen.

The kids aren't happy every second of the day, you
are not the perfect mother and that is really ok.

You are real and true,
You are safety and love.
You are laughter and joy,
And more of the above.

You are everything,
You are pure,
You are home,
You are crazy galore

You are not enough,
You never will be,
So release all the pressure,
And just be happy and free.

Just say

Spread your words like wings of love,
Compliments 'a plenty!
How many people can you make feel good - I bet
it's more than twenty!

'Your hair looks great!'
'I love your shoes'
'You look fantastic, have you lost weight'

When Ive felt low or sad, and someone stops to
chat, it really helps my mood and for this I am so
glad!

I promise when you do this, you change a persons
day...
With words of love and kindness, if you have a
thought - just say!

Musing thoughts

What are these thoughts flying around my head,
Are they real? Are they fact?
Perhaps they are just stories, I've made up instead.

They keep me up at night, they hassle me through
the day, what ifs and whys, could I have done
things a different way?!

These thoughts they'll pull you down. You must
take back control.
They are stories, you've made them up, stop losing
sleep going over and over it all.

Thoughts are thoughts, they don't control you.
Now hold the wheel and drive your own life
forward.

More thoughts

Heavy thoughts lay on your mind,
Holding you back,
Keeping you small

Release these thoughts,
They are not real,
Free yourself my love

Stories in your head,
No facts or evidence,
Keeping you up at night,
They really have no right

Release these thoughts,
They are not real,
Free yourself my love

Too much

To believe you're not enough, in this life it can be tough.
To believe you're too much,
Too sensitive, too loud, too much of everything and more.
Not enough, too much,
Where should I stand upon this floor.

Was I not enough, was I just too much? Maybe it wasn't me at all,
Maybe it just wasn't.
Maybe all these feelings come from outside. Maybe just maybe, it wasn't me at all.

Finding my feet

Finding my feet, finding my way
Discovering a new path, day by day.

My feet brush past the dew on the grass, new dirt
underfoot, it's an un walked path.

I don't run or sprint, sometimes I stop, I crouch
down to rest,
I breathe in the flowers and feel all the moments, I
always get up, and give it my best.

This path is un pathed, no ones been here before,
I look all around me, I study with awe.

With each careful step, destination unknown, I
turn to look back,
I admire how I've grown.

Take a deep breath, one foot in front of the other, I
raise up my wings and I know she was right, I can
hear my mums words, 'Go fly my darling'

Destination in sight!

The Mountain

The mountain of sobriety
It's not everyone's to climb,
We all face different struggles,
I guess alcohol was mine

'You didn't drink responsibly?'
'You didn't follow the rules?'
'How did you let this happen?'
'Well, shit this must be my fault!' - that inner critic
ridicules.

But here's the thing, the big news flash… that
alcohols a drug,
And for some of us, in just a flash, it pulls away the
rug.

We look up at the mountain,
My god it looks so high,
I'll never get up there,
I'd need wings to make me fly!

With every step and every fall,
I was damn sure that i'd fail!
I'd tumble down with brand new triggers, my
sobriety was frail!

Every time I got back up, new wisdom in my belt, I
tasted the life I wanted, I knew how good that felt.

Walls got built, foundations strong, with every craving squashed, they rear their heads from time to time, but pretty soon they're quashed.

Sobriety was a mountain, and once it felt too high, but I have the taste for climbing now,

So let's go touch that sky...

Goddess

Have you forgotten the power that you are? The force that you are? The goddess that you are?

You've been dampened down, made to feel less than, not enough - the mass production of cookie cutter beauty.

Perfect shape, perfect lips, perfect eyebrows - I'm so done, you're so done, we're so done!

It courses through your veins, the powers all within, that reflection in the mirror holds so much more, look deeper, see through discerning eyes.

The waves of pressure crash upon your back, but rise above them my darling, your beauty is within.

Within your strength, resilience. Within your heart, unconditional love. Within your mind, of curious thoughts.
Within your hands, of climbing higher.
Within your dreams, of your desires.
Within your aura, of comfort and hope.
Within your patience, holding space.
Within your arms, to hold on through storms.

That reflection holds nothing more than shallow perfections, look deeper, look within, hear your ancestors chants, you are more than this - stand tall and claim your place, carry your flame and be proud of who you are, all that you stand for and all that's to come.

Beauty is shallow, let love flow through.

Connection is key

I write it all down,
I throw it all out,
I pull out my pen,
I scream and I shout

I write down words of healing and fears, it's my
way of journaling, I've done this for years

Let's slow it down, what are you writing now?
What page are you on, what stage are you at?

A calm stage, of peace and pure ease. This stage is
my favourite, full of grace, I feel so ready, so ready
for it all.

I feel part of something, something truly great. I
feel connected to you, I'm connected to me, I find
connection is the key.

If my pain helps your pain, if you connect with my
words, then you're not alone, and you are not lost.

From a soul that's been through it, the up down
and round. I wrote these words out, I'd scream and
I'd shout.

Healing is messy, it's gritty and tough,
But you have to go through, not around or above.

Up way up high, down really low, Iv been there my friend, I have, so I know.

I'll be sitting right here, in this calm sea I'm on,
I'll hold out life jackets
If anyone needs one

I'll hold you, you hold me,
Never lost again, never lost out at sea.

A sea of faces, that we see but don't know, in the hustle bustle of the world, it can be a lonely road.

But I've said it before and I'll say it again,
connection, connection, connection is key.

The Women's Wellness Group
Upton Upon Severn

I'll sit with you

You cannot do it all,
You cannot always win,
The true joy is in the being,
Thats where you should begin.

If tomorrow seems to far,
Let's take today instead,
Just for today 'I am'
And then just rest your head

What actions can you take right now,
That improve your life tomorrow,
What changes can you make,
That do not bring you sorrow.

If you cannot do today,
Let's focus on this hour,
What is it you need right now,
Perhaps just take a shower.

Cleanse away those rushing thoughts,
Watch them leave you down the drain.
It's sometimes hard to see the light,
When you have that monkey in your brain.

If you cannot do this hour,
I'll sit with you my friend,
Because I've walked this road before,
And I know these feelings end.

Why do you silence your voice

When you don't speak up,
Your soul shrinks,
This I believe to be true.
When you stop yourself saying your thoughts, you
hold back the part that is you.

But what will they think, how will they view me, if
I hold my voice up and shout.
But my darling what if they love you? And that
you'd of have never found out!

Gentle steps

Take gentle steps,
Softly spoken words,
Let them flow through you,

Take small flutters,
Take tiny leaps,
Let them be who you are,

Gentle with your words,
Intentional with your steps,
Let them come for you

You are what you speak,
You do as you will,
Let them be them and you be you

Let's be small

Shall we be children,
Just for the day.

Let's forget all our worries,
And just simply play.

Let's sit in the grass and get our feet wet,
Let's spin and let's twirl, and get our needs met.

Let's nap, mid afternoon,
Let's eat what we want,
Let's frolic and swoon.

Swoon over dreams,
And plans that we have,
No thoughts of how, or worries what path.

It can't last forever, we're adults after all, but just
for today,
Let's just be small.

Risk the tide

Will she keep on walking,
Or will she run to shore?

Will she just start swimming,
Or run home and close the door?

Will she allow herself some grace,
To carve a path and make mistakes?

Will she let the ebb and flow take her dreams to
places far and wide

Or will she just stay safe, stay dry and not risk the
tide.

Rainbow

Dear rainbow, how long have you been there? How long did I not care?

I didn't see you at first because I was busy.

I was busy with life you see, it's really busy being me.

I have to work and be a mum, I have to give give give and sometimes there's no time for fun.

I was busy worrying about the dishes, I forgot to look up and make some wishes.

I was busy checking my phone, not realising I was becoming a drone.

I was busy working 9-5, it's what we are told to do - it's how we survive.

But dear rainbow now I see, I see so much of you, and in you I see me.

You are so bright, so beautiful and bold, and you do all of this without being told.

You stand out proud against the grey, and you stand out proud come what may.

You don't over think, or put yourself last. You don't come when it's time or leave really fast.

You are there, I looked up, I saw you today. Full of dreams of gold, and a promise they say.

Dear rainbow today I looked up and saw you against all the grey. Today I looked up and forgot my dismay.

I am me

Being accepted just as you are,
Throughout your life, headed so far

Being accepted for just being you,
Always be kind and always be true

Being accepted can sometimes hold weight, on our
thoughts, our dreams, ideas - a lot is at stake.

Being accepted won't always be,
This can feel hard, and shake up your thoughts, but
it shouldn't be given to much regard.

Being accepted can mean quite a lot,
But it shouldn't, you see,
It takes freedom and courage to say
'I am me'

To the WWDD Women, My Friends

To write down how I feel,
Well there isn't quite the words.
 I've nearly done a year,
The thought seems so absurd.
I felt the hand on alcohol, grasp me like a clasp. To
think of escaping that life, it truly made me gasp.
I didn't think I'd cope, for alcohol was my friend. It
always wrapped me up, and made those feelings
end.
But a friend it was not,
Although it tried to lie and lie,
It only ever worked out one way,
A way that made me cry.

I felt helpless, on the floor,
But I knew that I had more.
I knew that taking action,
There must be hope, there must be.

Be it just a glimmer,
Be it just a speck,
Something deep inside me,
Something had to check.

Check this wasn't it,
That there was more to life.
More ways to heal and cope,
And more than just this strife.

I'd pushed the button on my life,

It felt like no way out.
But that little inner child,
She screamed at me
She screamed you have to shout!

So I lay in bed and listened,
For she had more to say,
She knew this wasn't it,
She knew there was a way.

It wasn't pretty, easy or clear,
This path that lay ahead.
But I took it step by step,
Going back is not an option,
The thought filled me with dread.

I joined up in the group,
I was surrounded by support,
I'd never shared these deep dark thoughts, but
now I thought I ought.

And from it was my passage,
A new life that I could see.
There was no judgement here,
Only ever love for me.

The good the bad the ugly,
You guys you've seen it all.
You've bounced when I hit milestones,
You've caught me from the fall.

From such dark times to balance,

Thats more than I could ask,
I embrace all of this group,
I take on every task.

Back to basics,
Celebrate,
Catch the stories,
Get irate.

You hold the space for all,
You stopped me feeling small.
You guys are my foundation,
My friends, my rocks,
You keep me standing tall.

My heart is full of gratitude,
Reaching dreams I'd never dream,
I want to tell you all,
Just how much that means.

Like a Queen

Today I'll spend the day like a queen,
I'll pin up my hair, and polish my shoes,
I'll put on some lipstick and worry not of the blues

Today is only bright sky,
Only clear thoughts,
Only calm communication,

For today I hold my peace as paramount. I hold my self as priority.

Today I worry not of tomorrow,
Today I worry not of yesterday,
For today I am the queen,
I am special, pure,
Staying calm,
Being free,
Today is the day I prioritise me.

Maybe Tomorrow

Maybe one day,
One day but not today.
It might one day flow and live and breath
And maybe it would be right, to write,
But not today,
Not on this day,
But maybe tomorrow
Maybe when the seas not so salty,
And the airs not so fresh,
And the trees no longer sway in the wind,
Maybe then,
But not today.
Not this day, this one right now.
Maybe one day though,
One day soon,
When the light comes from just the moon,
The old love songs no longer swoon,
And the world is quiet, not any sound,
But not today, not this day.
But maybe tomorrow,
Time will tell,
As it rolls the tomorrows into today's,
And we wait for time,
Thats yet to stay,
But maybe tomorrow's day will be today, and not
tomorrow, and tomorrow's me will tell tales of love
and sorrow,
And as I write and hold the pen, it flows and lives,
and maybe then,
Maybe tomorrow,

But not today.
Today will soon become yesterday,
And in that space,
Dreams will stay,
And if tomorrow should not come,
Today was the day,
Not some day soon,
Today is the day,
Tomorrows is yesterday,
Yesterday's tomorrow,
For times one thing,
We cannot borrow.
Maybe today is the day.

Rest

Sometimes the days feel big, to big to really hold.
On days of nothingness, stillness, silence that feels
so loud. Because rest is to be lazy,
And the feelings are so strong,
You cannot rest there is no time,
But that's where you are wrong.
You see the world won't stop,
And nothing will crash down,
You are allowed to sit,
And rest,
And do nothing,
Nothing at all.
This isn't being lazy,
That's just in your head,
An echoed voice,
But it's untrue,
Turn that voice right down.
Permission just to rest,
It's needed from within,
Permission to just be,
It's the only way to win.

I See You

I see you,
Sitting there wondering why you can't seem to
grasp it
Left feeling foggy with another failed attempt at
moderate drinking,
Normal drinking, being normal,
Stopping at one,
Questioning why and what is wrong with me.
I see you, I've been you.

I don't drink everyday so there is no problem,
I don't drink in the morning ,
I'm being dramatic,
I'm always dramatic,
It must just me,
I'll just carry on...

Back on the hamster wheel,
All is forgotten,
I'll be fine this time,
I'm just being silly,
Feeling hungover,
Feeling low,
Feeling these feelings with nowhere to go.

But this times not different,
It's just like the last,
Having one drink and then
Boom - it's so fast
Well I'll have another;

I don't have a problem

Look around! Everyone drinks everyone does!
Everyone gets hungover it's normal - this fuzz

Because what would life be without pouring a
wine, chatting with friends, this is stupid. I'm fine!

But you're not fine, are you?
I've been you,
And deep down you know -

That this, well it's all for just for show.

Because deep down it doesn't feel fine,
It feels incessant, deceptive, it's not just a wine.

But maybe, just maybe,
This is the time.

Its ok, it really is

Sometimes we find it in the sky, the glimmer of the
sun shining past the grey clouds, sometimes we
find it in the time passing conversations
throughout the day, the knowing smiles of souls
unlocking connections from times gone by,
sometimes we find it in moments, fleeting ones,
soulful ones, long over due ones, always ever
present, always ever flowing. Always the answers,
questions sometimes unknown. Always the truth,
always the lie.
Forever within us, forever present.
But then sometimes we can't find it, only clouds
and fog, and your soul feels lost and heavy, the
tears, they fall.
But you know it's not forever, you know that this
shall pass,
For love is always there, and the hope will come
back,
don't give up and don't give in,
for there is nothing that you lack.
Nothing to win and nothing to gain,
You will get through,
Search deep in this pain

What's the cost

I wish we could just soak it up,
Every single drop,
As I sit here with a heavy chest,
Watching murder documentaries,
The callus actions from a man,
Who found brute strength within a can,
His love ran out in beads of sweat,
The hangover must feel so cold,
As now he's killed someone he loved,
And he's lost his life from times of old.
I didn't think I did that,
I really didn't mean to,
How he wept,
But how he kept,
And how they then unlikely slept.

But what about the kids,
The trauma they must hold,
What about what's left behind,
Such destruction left within its wake,
This tale, well it is getting old.

Lives destroyed by something we,
Are sold to being pleasure,
A poison that we freely drink,
Enjoy it at our leisure

But what about the cost,
Not the cost of just the drink,
The cost to lives across the world,

Destroyed within a blink.

I wish we could wake up,
And see through all its lies,
This alcohol, well it's a drug,
Open up your eyes

The cost, the fun, the happiness,
 it soaks it up so fast,
We look back to the memories,
Forgotten, in the past.

It's overlooked you see,
Accepted by the mass,
But a lot of what did happen,
Lives that have been lost,
It took them for the pleasure,
So what really is the cost.

'The woman I am becoming thanks the women I was for not giving up'

The Light

The most important light,
Is the one you cannot see,
The one that shines in you,
The one that shines in me,

The one that breaks through the long dark night,
The one that shines through,
no matter how hard the fight

The light in your soul,
The light that you shine,
You should keeping shining yours,
And I'll keep shining mine.

Some Days

Some days are heavy,
Some days weigh less,
Some days your heart, beats right through your
chest.
Some days are full,
And some days are dull,
Some days you feel every direction you're pulled.
Some days are funny,
Some days are sad,
Some days all you can feel is just feeling glad,

Glad that you made it,
Through all the days,
The good ones, the bad ones,
The come with what mays,

Glad you remember that
This shall too pass,
The good and the bad,
To watch for the glimmers
Whenever you're sad.

Some days are heavy,
Some days weigh less,
But you show up for them all,
And you try your best.

Your best is enough,
Your best is what's true,
Through everyday,

Just keep being you.

You who is loved for all that you do,
All that you are,
Just keep being you.

Dreams

To live a life not filled with dreams,
Well surely it is lost.
The fear within,
Keeping you safe,
But really at what cost.

To live a life not speckled in risk,
Opportunity's do arise,
But they merely get missed.

To live a life with fear of change,
Never able to manoeuvre,
Or rearrange.

To live a life,
With no dreams,
Well my dear this is no life at all,
If you can dream it then it can be real,
And know the stars will catch you,
Should you ever fall.

You'll find what is true

If you fall to the bottom,
If you fall to your knees,
If you feel defeated and low,
Like you may just give up,
Look to within,
It's where you must go.

It's where you must go,
To muster the strength,
The strength you've forgotten,
Got lost in the fog.

It's in there you know,
She's right there waiting,
The girl you once were,
When nothing felt too big,
And you didn't feel so small.

Take a look in the mirror,
Take a deep breath,
Wipe the tears away,
And remember.

You must remember her.

Not to be her again,
This time much stronger,
Using this pain to push down the walls,
To much brighter times,
That future,

It calls.

She's in there you know,
You've met in your dreams,
She's the one who's got it all,
Her smile, it beams

Muster and gather,
And take a deep breath,
Take it fast, take it slow,
The choice, well it's yours.

But you are still her,
And she is still you,
And with love and with kindness,
You'll find what is true

Me too

My two favourite words,
Me too.

Me too is more than just letters,
Me too to me sounds like this,
I'm taking the mask of and admitting defeat,
I stand on no pedestal,
Only my feet,
I also feel that I'm not enough,
That I get overwhelmed with the smallest of stuff.
Me too to me sounds like standing there bare,
With no airs or graces,
Just me with my share,
My share of worries, my share of pain,
My share of wisdom, my share of gain.
Me too to me has sounds of soft words,
A feeling of comfort, not perfection in herds.
It's not met with advice, or words to help fix, it
meets you right where you are, in whatever mix.
Me too to me feels like safety and love,
To be who you are,
And believe it's enough.

Me too, my two favourite words,
Shared between strangers or friends,
In any part of the world,
Me too, Me too,
in any time or space,
Means 'I see you, I love you, and judgement holds
no place'

Best Friend

I have this person, she's my best friend.
Last night she gave the kitchen a once over before
she went to bed, she was tired, but she knew I'd
have a better day to wake up to a clear kitchen.

She gets me up super early, she knows I have a
better day when I do this, sometimes she suggests
yoga, sometimes we just sit in the quite with a
cuppa.

She reminds me that thoughts are just thoughts,
that we don't have to act on or pay mind to all of
them.

She reminds me that I can be uncomfortable, and
whispers in my my ear tales of growth that have
come before from these uncomfortable moments.

She puts lovely fresh sheets on my bed and always
puts my favourite pyjamas on the pillow, she
knows that it makes me smile come bed time.

She quickly squashes thoughts of ever drinking;
you see she sat with me whilst we removed it, and
that took a lot, but she sat through all the
moments, she reminds me how alcohol is not a
friend of ours, I'm always grateful for this.

She runs me nice baths, with bubbles and candles,
and picks my favourite books out to read, often

books of learning and inspiration, she knows these are my favourite.

My best friend I speak of, well she is me.

I decided a while back that this life is 100% my responsibility, and that being my own best friend, one with words of kindness and compassion, support and encouragement, would be far more powerful in my life, than having that inner critic take centre stage.

I think it's important to be your own best friend, I think its important to treat yourself exactly as you would a best friend. Be your biggest supporter, your loudest cheerleader.

I thought I'd remind you, incase you had forgotten to invite your best friend back in lately.

The Ships

The ships are safe in the harbour,
But that's not what they're built for.
To step out of your comfort zone,
Can leave you feeling quite unsure,
But ships are safe in the harbour,
But that's not what they're built for,
It might feel safer, no stormy seas,
No worry of judgement to leave unease,
Yes the ships are safe in the harbour,
But that's not what they're built for,
And deep down you know, as do I,
Setting sail is the only cure.

Weird Weirdo

Just be weird and wonderful,
just be weird weirdo,
Being normal, that's not you!
Be weird and wonderful all day long, and sing out
loudly the words of your song.

Be wonderfully weird every damn day,
Say what you mean and mean what you say.
Just be a weirdo, that couldn't care less,
If they laugh or they smirk at the way that you
dress.

At the way that you speak, the way that you feel,
The way you create, and all you express
I'll tell you a secret,
It's because they're less!

Just be a weirdo, a wonderful one,
and fall back in love,
With the girl in the mirror,
Who said 'enough is enough'

The Dance of the Dragon

There is a dance of the dragon in my memories,
The kind of memory that you aren't sure if it was a
reality, a dream, or a picture of your imagination.

Perhaps it's from a past life,
Perhaps I have danced with the dragon before,
The bright colours, the reds, the fire, the sense of
togetherness.

Perhaps this memory is not just mine, but also
mine from a life lived before me.
Perhaps my soul had a life before this one, and
perhaps I danced with the dragon then.

Years ago, when I first met my husband, we visited
a flea market local to us. It was there that I found a
beautiful amethyst set in a sterling silver snake
ring. I adored this ring, I didn't take it off for a year
or more. But when I did take it off, I never found it
again.

In Chinese tradition each year is named after one
of 12 different animals of the Chinese zodiac: Rat,
ox, tiger, rabbit, dragon, snake, horse, goat,
monkey, rooster, dog and pig.

The order of the years comes from a story about a
race across a river which was set by the Jade
Emperor.

The animals all wanted the year to be named after them so they competed to cross the river the fastest and, through cunning, the rat won.

Then the other animals got to be named after a year in the order they finished the race. There is a 12 year cycle of animal names.

This year, we are in the year of the Snake. The snake, which is the sixth animal, represents wisdom, intuition and transformation.

Snakes shed there skin, they transform. They release what no longer serves them.

I feel transformation ahead, I hear the echos of wisdom from my intuition to trust in the universe, in myself.

This morning, after a difficult few days, facing some truths that have been masked, that my brain has kept me safe from, I found my snake ring that I had lost all those years ago.

I put it on, I felt the calm from the amethyst, I felt the power of the symbol.

I'm ready to face the difficult to invite the new, to shed old behaviours that no longer serve me.

I'm ready now, to dance with the dragon once more. To feel the power of change, to release into the flaming breath as the dragon engulfs me whilst I transform, shedding my skin, listening to my intuition.

Sometimes change is uncomfortable, change usually is. But sometimes these signs are all around us, to trust, and keep going, to dance with the dragon once more.

And on we go...

Sunday

On Sundays we meander more,
We worry less,
We take deeper breaths,
We take softer steps.

On Sundays we notice more,
We notice the wind in our hair,
We notice the shadows on the floor,
The ripples in the water on the Sunday stroll, the
leaves dancing, on the beautiful big trees, the birds
songs, the nice cups of tea.

On Sundays we take it slower, take it kinder, take it
softer.

It's a day for meanders,
For bright sunshine walks,
For bubbles in the bath,
For gentle roaring fires.

It's a day for softly spoken words,
Slow cooked roasts,
Comfy blankets and your favourite pyjamas.

It's a day for the soul,
A day where the world slows down and we all
catch our breath.

Tomorrow on the busy Monday, with places to be
and deadlines to meet,

I'll remember my softer Sunday,
I'll remember the bright sunshine on my face, the
bubbles in the bath and the warmth of the fire,

And I'll be glad I took my Sunday,
Softly in my stride,
Whilst the world slowed down together,
We enter into the new week,
with our Sunday on our side.

Keep Swimming

I can't write a poem on this one,
I can't write it all away,
It feels another huge step back,
It feels lost in darkness and dismay

I thought it was all pink clouds,
Nice walks, And all that good stuff.
But the skies gone awful grey right now,
And I can't paint this mask on any more.

I want to swim back to shore,
The water feels deep,
To deep for me,
Only unknown beneath,

but I must catch my breath,
Tread my legs,
And keep swimming a little more.

Sunflowers (unfinished) *explicit*

I was writing a poem about sunflowers tonight, it was pretty good. I was going to share it with you, anyway, it's unfinished right now. Whilst writing I had the Vicky Pattison Deep fake sex tape programme on channel 4 on in the background.

I sat getting angrier and angrier for these women this had happened to. How dare they. How fucking dare they. I felt rage, deep rage in my stomach for these women.

Then I instantly wanted to remove every image, every video, everything of my family, of myself, from the internet that ever existed.

But the stubbornness inside of me said no. Why should I. Why the hell should I not share, not post, not embrace the beautiful parts of social media. The parts where we comment on other women's pictures because they look beautiful, because they achieved something wonderful, because they need a friend or some kind words. Why should I erase us from the internet , that has some wonderful place in our world, just because of these sick and twisted people.

When terror attacks happen and we stop going to concerts, to football matches, to fireworks displays, stop travelling- they win.

And when we erase ourselves from the internet -
they win.

F**k that.

The only way to not let that happen is to keep
LIVING. Keep enjoying. Keep sharing. Keep being.
And most importantly - Keep talking. Keep raising
awareness. Keep being true to ourselves, our
authenticity, our absolute right to keep on. Because
for every person that might think this is somehow
acceptable, somehow not completely immoral,
there's a million other decent and beautiful people
that do the right thing. That live their life doing no
harm to others, helping people out, sharing kind
words on a picture, on a memory, on some shared
joy.

Let's not delete ourselves,
Let's keep being proud,
Let's keep loving, keep living, keep enjoying our
lives.

To shrink, to delete, to avoid is to let them win.

Not today, not tomorrow, not ever.

You lose, there's too many good people for you to
ever win.

So I'll finish my poem about sunflowers, and I'll
remember how they stand tall, how they live in the

brightest of yellow, holding no apologies for
showing up in the world. How they grow to great
heights, how they always look for the light,
Because it's always, always there.
And then how they bask,
Beautiful, open,
In the sunshine.
And they pay no mind to the weeds beneath them.
They win, the sunflower always wins.

A letter to myself, on the hard days…

Oh no. The thoughts are back.
Why are they so loud!
I've done my very best today,
Why can't I just feel proud.

I didn't solve world hunger,
Or cure a big disease,
But I did get out of bed today,
Is that not enough to please?

Overthinking thoughts,
That I'm not good enough,
Full imposter syndrome,
They bounce around, it's rough!

What's the cure to this,
I sit here and I think.
A solution to most problems,
Used to be to pour a drink

But I don't do that anymore,
Best decision ever made!
but these thoughts need to be dealt with,
To step out from this shade

This shade is just a shadow,
Of these dark dark thoughts,
We've conquered them before my love,
So think back, dig deep,
you're just feeling out of sorts

Maybe just kind words,
Or maybe take some rest,
Make sure you do remember,
You do your very best

This feeling it won't last,
It never ever has,
Tomorrows a new day,
You know that this will pass

Don't take haste in this,
Don't allow it to sink deep,
This is just a feeling,
But not one that you'll keep

So dry your eyes,
Nothings lost,
Don't burn out,
It's to bigger cost

Listen to your gut,
It's always always right,
You need some words of kindness
not these words of spite

Allow yourself to take a rest,
You've done enough,
You've done your best

You'll be ok believe me,
I know this to be true,

In know this in my heart,
Because I, my dear, am you.

The Nomad

I heard this said tonight,

'The more comfort you are willing to sacrifice, the more access to the world you will have'

Now this man was talking about nomad camping. But he has a point doesn't he.

Get uncomfortable.
Being comfortable keeps us stagnant. Stuck even. Sticking with what we know, leaves a lot of stuff out there that we'll never learn. And that's a shame. Especially as we are big learning machines.

I don't think the aim in life is to sit still. To just be comfortable. To never explore further into the world, into ourselves, into the notion that there is more to see, more to learn, more to create.

There is a time for sitting still, it is limited. There is a time for moving forward, also limited.
But one thing is for sure, and that is that you are limitless, and balance of being still and moving, remains the key

The only limits in your life are set by you. Limiting beliefs. Limiting relationships. Limiting friendships. Limiting goals.

Don't you want more, don't you want to touch the grass of foreign lands,
To glide through the desert on horseback,
To dive into the oceans of the big deep blue. To discover who you are, what you're made of. To challenge, to explore. To go deeper, to strive to become the best version of yourself, in authenticity and power.

Don't you want to be all you can be,
To achieve all you can achieve,
To see what's out there,
Waiting for you.

To sit in comfort is to sit stagnant,
To get uncomfortable is to stand in growth.

So stand in it my friend.

Stand under the stars, Under the moonlit nights, and dream, and when you wake from your slumber,

Go get it,
All of it.
Every last desire of your heart.

It won't always feel comfortable,
But it will always feel worth it.

I did it for ME

What makes you happy?

What brings you joy?

What makes you smile from ear to ear, like a child
with a brand new toy.

What brings you peace?

What brings you calm?

Just go take a break and do it,
It really does no harm.

The washing will wait,
The dusting will too,

There is always time for joy,
Time just for you.

Just let your hair down,
It's ok to do less,
You've done more than enough,
And mess is just mess.

Be a bit silly,
And dance in the rain,
Don't wait 'till it's over,
To say 'if I had my time again'

Perhaps I'd do less,
Perhaps I'd do more,
More to bring joy,
Less time sweeping the floor

The floor makes no memories,
No none at all,
But it's great to dance on,
When you're acting the fool

Cherish the smiles,
The love and warm hugs,
You don't need a reason,

It's 'Joy' just because!

Life is to short,
So live it with Glee,

And if anyone asks, say

'I did it for ME'

Maybe the world needs a hug

Maybe the world needs a hug,
Or a cup of tea from it's favourite mug.

Maybe the world needs some love,
A moment of guidance sent from above.

Maybe the world needs a friend,
Someone to be there, right to the end.

Maybe the world needs kind words,
Sending them down on the wings of the birds.

Maybe the world needs a shoulder to cry on, a
place to lean when all hope feels gone.

Maybe the world needs something that's true,
Something authentic,
Something from you.

Prayers up high and roots down deep,
Go create,
Something the world could keep.

Self Love

One day I looked in the mirror and decided to be
free.
One day I looked in the mirror and decided to love
me.
One day it took all that I had
To look at my reflection, and to feel glad.
One day I scrolled down through my phone,
And saw all the things I do not own.
One day I scrolled through all the posts,
And compared the likes, Who had the most.
One day I searched up high and low to be like her,
to have her glow.
One day I forgot,
That it's not real,
It's really not.

One day I chose to love me more,
To leave comparisons at the door.
One day I put away the phone,
And looked around at all I own.

Somedays I do all the above,
So I try to remember,
To Choose self love.

What If

Stepping out onto the ice,
Worried it might crack.

The thoughts of fear looming near,
Weighing heavy on your back.

What if I can't do it,
What if the ice does crack,
What if I fail, tumble and fall,
What if...
What if ...
'Fear likes to keep us small'

But what if you just shoot your shot,
Give it your all,
All that you've got.

What if you just give it a go,
And squash that fear deep down below,

What would happen if you fail?
You'd get back up,
You would prevail,

So what really is it holding you back,
Keeping you stuck,
Living in lack.
If its a fear, that's deep down within,
Then my darling you must have forgotten,
You're also able to swim.

Sat around the table

I've been thinking a lot today about what we bring to the table. What I bring to the table. That saying 'what are you bringing to the table', it seems to have been a theme throughout my day to re hear this phrase over and over in my head.

But what if we bring nothing to the table. What if we sometimes we just sit at the table, with not even words to offer.

Sometimes we arrive at the table with our hands full of gifts for our families and communities, gifts of smiles and kind words, gifts of favours and flowers. Gifts of a helping hand or a word of wisdom - or a wonderful hug with a hot cup of tea.

But sometimes we don't, we show up with bare hands, tired souls, nothing to offer other than ourselves - our very vulnerable and unmasked selves; and I think that's ok.

I guess we all go through seasons, ever changing moods, hormones, life's challenges, the ups and the downs.

Sometimes we have much to offer, and sometimes we have nothing at all.

We are all ever changing, ever growing. It's endless, the wheels of life.

I think with true friendships, and unconditional family, these people don't care what you bring to the table, they just want you sat at it.

And that, I believe, is one of the biggest blessings in life, not what we or others bring to the table, but that we get to sit at the table, with no conditions and no judgement.

Who are the people sat around your table? Send them some love.

Happy New Year

What if we go in with no expectations,
And creep gently through the door.
What if we stop making false promises,
That makes us feel like we need to be more.

What if there is no pop of the fizz,
And we just rest our heads,
Knowing there's nothing we'll miss,

What if we tip toe quietly through,
Accepting that, you are just you.

You hold the power,
You hold the key,
You make the choices,
And you can be free.

Free of the pressure to join in at all.
Free of the wonders of having it all.

What if we just creep quietly through,
With no other promise,
Accept to love 'you'.

The Intention

The intention that sits on the tip of your tongue,
The one that comes with no effort at all,
The intention that feels deep within,
The one that you dream when the moonlight is
dim.

The intention that fills your deepest desires,
The one that feels up high, and higher and higher.

The one that is sat on the tip of your tongue, the
dreams that you dreamt when you were still
young.

The ones that you stopped daring to dream, they
felt to far fetched, to ever be seen.

The intentions get written, out to be seen, placed
in the unknown,
Just daring to dream.

New moon in the sky,
See my written out dreams,
You know me so well,
You know what this means...

Sit with it

Sit with it.
Sit with the notions, the itching of the skin.
Sit with the fear, the one that's deep within.
Sit with the tears, streaming down your face.
This won't last forever my love,
There is only you in this race.

They say this too shall pass,
And you know this to be true.
They say you hold the answers,
They're right, it's all in you.

Sit with it my love,
This un comfort, it won't last.
This will soon be just a memory,
One that's in the past.

So sit with it,
Sit with it my love,
It's holds some dear message,
Surround it with your love

Tangled lights still shine

I hope you understand,
I really hope you do,
I hope you understand,
That you're enough,
Just being you.

When Christmas lights are tangled,
They still shine just as bright.
Sometimes we get tangled,
But that's perfectly alright.

You don't have to be perfect,
No one really is.
Everything will be ok,
it always always is.

If the day does not bring joy,
If you're feeling close to tears,
Just no that that's ok,
There's no need for merry cheers.

If you want to stay in bed,
Stay curled up in a ball
Then I think that's just fine,
It's Christmas after all.

You do you tomorrow,
You put yourself first.
Whatever brings some comfort,
No need to feel rehearsed.

Christmas is just one day,
and tangled lights still shine,
You do you tomorrow,
That will be just fine.

*I wrote this for Catherine Kings, my wonderful
friend . Love you today, tomorrow, and always*

Happy Christmas

They are coming over the hill,
I try to send them back
But I can feel the darkness looming,
Heavier than Santa's sack.

I can feel the pressure building,
Around us so much joy,
Yet here I lay in bed again,
Not able to enjoy

The lights they twinkle on,
The decorated tree
But these all consuming thoughts,
Weigh heavy down on me.

Have I done enough,
The voices they get loud,
Will everyone be happy
Have I done enough to make them proud

Christmas can be hard,
the pressure is so vast
The world spins round and round
The demands come thick and fast

They say it doesn't matter,
What sits beneath the tree,
They say it really doesn't,
So why can I not see...

That Christmas is just Christmas,
It's just another day.
No one really remembers presents,
Please remember what I say,

It matters how we love,
It matters how we speak,
It matters what we do,
To make others feel less bleak.

It matters that we feel enough,
It matters that we rest,
It matters that we're ok,
We do our very best.

We try so very hard,
We really do enough,
Make sure you do remember,
That Christmas can be tough

So cut yourself some slack,
Give yourself a break,
I promise you - you are enough...

So sit back, and grab some cake.

Next Chapter

Every story, every page, every line yet to write.
Every story must find it's beginning, its middle and
its end

What would a story be without some lessons, some
smiles and some tears along the way

The suspense, the next page turn, a great story is
not for the faint hearted

A great story holds great strength,
The strength to turn the page,
And keep writing

For we shall never know what happens next, if we
do not take out our pens, and write the line, take
the action, and choose 'what's next'

You cannot hand someone else the pen,
For they could never read the tales of your heart,
or the depths of your soul, this is your story, you
hold the pen

So write the next line we must,
For this story is not over,
And I am ready for my next chapter.

I looked

I looked for the magic button,
I looked for the magic pill,
I searched all over for the off switch,
Falling further down the hill.

I reached for moderation,
I'd hoped in desperation,
That I'd become a normal drinker,
A magical creation.

Created in my mind,
Yet in reality does not exist.
She doesn't drink the red wine slowly,
By the fireplace,
Taking sips

As when temptation came,
I for sure gave in,
A heavy day,
A repressed emotion,
A celebration,
A grief,
A joy,
A holiday, with pumpkins or with prancer,

Well wine was always my answer.

For many many years I searched externally,
There has to be a cure,
An easy fix,

For sure.

But down the hill I fell,
Mental health was on the floor,
Another 3am wake up,
More sickness,
This was hell.

I had to go within,
I had to be my cure,
To fight back to all these demons,
And keep them from my door.

One Year

Remove the shame and ask for help,
Time the cravings,
Cry and shout,
Journal all the thoughts,
Write the poems too,
Discover brand new parts of me,
Beautiful, patient, calm, and true.

I'm not the old me,
For now she has gone,

She's watching from a star

With tears in her eyes she watches me leave into
the new and the unknown,
It's down to her that I am here,
The failed attempts were not fails, not one,
They are the very foundations that I stand upon.

This brand new milestone that I reach, I have to let
her go,
She is my past,
She is my pain,
She is my blood sweat and tears as I have played
this game.

But there was no magic button,
There was no magic pill,

It was my inner strength,

My fight for life,
That got me up this hill.

One year today,
Forever to go,
With no regrets,
And on I go.

Leave the light on

On the landing,
In the hall,
A flickering candle,
I'll light them all

Look to my window
For you will see
A landing light,
Left on from me

The light is mine
And now yours too,
I've felt the darkness
Just like you

If it feels dark
Inside your head
Overwhelmed with worries
Or filled with dread

If it feels like
You are alone,
Like nobody's there,
Nobody's home

Know this my friend,
These feelings end.
But just for right now,
While you can't find your torch,

Take a deep breath
And look for my porch

You will see a light,
It always stays on,
For ones feeling alone,
Till the darkness has gone.

If we all shone a light
For ones who are lost,
Left the lamp burning,
For paths we have crossed

If we all left on
Our landing light,
Wouldn't it be
Such a wonderful sight

Perfection

Sometimes I think we're all chasing the same picture, the one that glows softly through our screens at night. The perfect kitchen. The perfect family. The perfect life. The marble work tops with golden taps, that catch the light like water, sprayed in Purdy and fig. White walls that never knew a sticky fingerprint. A candle burning neatly beside a bowl of untouched lemons, as if the scent of citrus could hold the family together.

We scroll, we save and we sigh. We measure our own lives against the stillness of someone else's photograph, wondering how they do it, how their mornings seem so calm. But I want to remind you of something. Behind every photo there's a pile of washing just out of frame, a shout smothered by a filter, a parent balancing too many dreams on too little sleep.

And sometimes, behind the perfection, theirs a child. A quite one, old enough to know not to ask again, but young enough to still hope you'll look up.

A pre teen who hovers in the doorway, still unable to create the conversation with confidence but who so desperately needs a cuddle, and a moment of connection. Real connection, completely un masked, un instagram worthy moments of perfectly imperfect connection. Not needing to earn attention through achievement or image. Without our presence and consistence, they drift, they drift into the screens, into friends who listen, into worlds that don't ask them to tidy up their emotions in order to be seen.

Ive been in houses that are belonging between the pages of magazines, silent, scented, everything organised and in its rightful place. And i've been in homes that hum with life. Where the kitchen table is scarred with stories, Where the fridge door is a collage of drawings, reminder notes and half wiped fingerprints. Where the washing basket overflows, but so does the laughter. Those are the homes that stay with me. The ones that imprint on our souls as memories. Like my nans imperfect lounge and cucumber sandwich summer holidays.

We spend so much time polishing the surfaces of our lives that we forget to live in them. Oh my how I would love a marble top kitchen, it is beautiful, but it doesn't remember birthdays, or catch tears, or smell like pancakes on a Sunday morning, made on a ridiculous tacky crepe maker from B&M. It cant tell the story of the child who still sets the table crookedly, or the parent who sat down to listen, despite being tired after a long day.

They say comparison is the thief of joy, I wrote a poem about just that, but its also the thief of connection. It steals eye contact. It steals bedtime stories. It steals the messy, perfectly ordinary moments that stitch love into the fabric of our days.

Maybe perfection isn't what we've been told it is. Maybe its not the gleam of order, but instead the glow of belonging. Maybe its ok for the floor to be sticky if it means the you get to be in the same room as the laughter. Maybe its ok for the photos to be blurred, because life rarely stands still.

Love doesn't live in marble countertops.
It lives in the crumbs, the chaos, in the noise, in the overfilled washing baskets, the unmade beds, the un matching pyjamas.
It lives in the child that is seen, loved unconditionally, wrapped up in imperfections.
It lives in the perfectly imperfect versions of us.
It lives in the tears and the cuddles.
It lives in the acceptance.
It lives in our hearts, whether its perfect to not.

Remember to live in it. All of it.

*'Maybe the journey isn't about becoming anything.
Maybe its about unbecoming everything that isn't
really you'*

Paulo Coelho

The Author

Did you think it might come true?
Or just assume you'd fail?
Did you picture a victory lap,
The certificate in the mail?

Did you visualise the win
Feel how it would rise within?
Or does victory whisper defeat,
And you just took your seat
Never thinking it could be you,
Never believing that was true.

Did you assume that you are less,
And with self-belief you shouldn't mess?
Never thinking *it could be me,*
No, not it could be, it will be,
It has to be.

For in this life, we do not fail.
We learn. We bend. We move.
With nothing left to prove.

Did you assume it could be you,
And do all that you could do?
If you did, then really,
You won.
You had the fun.

There is no fail,
Only mis-takes

Moments to retake, reshape, remake.

And really, it means nothing at all,
Except the love,
The joy
That's what counts.

So I think, really, you made it.
Whatever *it* is for you.
Whatever the dream,
It all comes true.

Because we are what we believe.
We are who we deceive.
We are what we create.
We are who we berate.

So really, we are the author
Of every chapter,
Every tale.

So when you think about it...
There really are no fails.

Or Just Be You

We can hope to be taller, slimmer, smaller,
We can strive to be better, brighter, smarter
We can want to have hair thats longer,
Straighter, smoother
We can desire to be more tanned, less freckled,
More flawless
We can yearn to be younger, older, wiser
We can wish to be wittier, bubblier, louder

Or you could just be you

You could just love you, accept you, protect you,
Just simply be, you.

Isn't that the biggest injustice we do,
To wish to be anything other than true.

Forever

I think we'd always find each other,
In any universe,
In any dimension,
In any scale of time,
In any form of being,
And I think we always have,
I think we've always been,
And I think we always will be.
I think in every life time,
I'll always find you,
And you'll always find me.
So when I say forever,
It's bigger than just the notion of this forever,
of some romantic tale,
It's every forever,
For ever.

Written for my husband, Sam

Medusa

It's a myth, they said,
when they looked at Medusa
snakes for hair,
eyes that could turn a man to stone.
Monster, they called her.
Evil, they said.
But nobody talks about the reason that snakes
grew from her head.

See, before the curse,
she was beauty,
she was power wrapped in softness,
Poise wrapped in being,
she was a woman
and that was enough to make them afraid.

It's a myth, they said.
But maybe she's still here.
Maybe she's that woman in the office
who speaks too loud,
too sure,
too much.
The one they call *intimidating*
when what they mean is *honest.*

Maybe she's that girl who walks home at night
keys between her fingers,
heart steady,
eyes forward,
turning fear into armour.

It's a myth, they said,
but myths don't die, they evolve.
They grow new faces,
new names,
new ways of saying *no more.*

Medusa doesn't live in temples now
she lives in mirrors.
In every reflection that whispers,
you are not the monster they made you out to be.

It's a myth, they said,
but I say it's a memory.
A warning.
A prophecy.

Because every time someone rises
from their own ruin
and calls it rebirth
that's Medusa,
breathing again,
Walking this Earth

Kitchen Disco

In the music we listen,
We dance,
The echoes of the words drip feeding our soul -
Pure dopamine through the beat
And down to our feet
And we have a shit day and we yearn for escape,
To take the thoughts of stress away
And that's really all that it is,
A creation from one heart to yours
To clear the day
To take a restart
Reset the brain and fire and aim
And hearing the beat,
Getting up from your seat
And releasing the day,
I think it's called a kitchen disco,
Better with friends but wild alone,
Done in pyjamas or your bestest of clothes
And it feels pretty good to shake of the day,
And not worry for wobbles
And lose the dismay

A kitchen disco you say,
Well then I'm on my way.

The Fog

I cannot move this fog,
No matter the kind words, the gentle reminders,
the soft moments of support,
It feels immovable. Unbearable. Intractable.
The weight of the black dog,
The heaviness of the fog,
The dampness of the tear soaked top,
The emptiness,
Un United,
Un controlled
And surely
Un deserved.
I didn't ask for this, nor do I want to feel this way,
Nor do I feel deserving of this weighted dismay,
For the weight I cannot carry.
The noise I cannot take,
The silence is not golden,
I fear that I may break.

The mind so very fragile,
And there was no straw to break the camels back,
It was simply built up over time,
The pressure of the race,
The one against only myself,
Yet still, I lack the pace.

I want to leave on words hope,
Yet this feels so far away,
So for now, I will just leave,
And just get through today.

Mushrooms & Mindset

Life's full of little mushrooms
Little feathers
Little insects
Of colour
So much colour
Little acorns
Little moments
Little laughter bursts
Little fears

Some we win,
Some we lose,
But as for mindset,
We get to choose

And so we know
This to shall pass

So on we go

What Doesn't Kill Me

It's an obsession, just to survive.
As if all the words ever written
must pass through my mouth...
As if the universe itself
pulls my head upward.

I look to the crowd
but deeper than that.
Sometimes... I walk against it.
Even when it's hard.

I passionately speak
of this earth that's so full,
and of surviving in a time
when technology thrives...
When creation doesn't always come from the heart
but sometimes
from a phone that has somehow grown smart.

Still, this drive shows even in darkness.
When lifting my head
from a tear-soaked pillow
feels like wrestling, the heaviest black dog.

There was a book about this.
I read it.
Maybe you did too.

But still
we lifted our heads.

Time and again.

Dragged treacle-stuck shoes, down to the kitchen,
turned off the news,
made some toast,
left the crumbs on the side.

Because we,
we have this drive
to survive.

I've battled the darkness.
The darkest of thoughts.
I've felt the emptiness,
felt too fragile for sunlight's glare.
felt invisible in mirrors I faced
wore my emptiness instead of skin
felt too hollow to stand in the light
felt unworthy of any future in sight.

I've grappled with self-love,
chased it, fought it,
until finally
I could run with wolves.

Wild.
Free.
Finally able
to fully love me.

Life is raw.
Real.

Fun.

And we desire to keep going,
until we are done.

What doesn't kill me...

Well, it Better run.

Sometimes the wagon is too high,
The horses go to fast,
Your saddle doesn't feel steady,
And so the doubt does cast

Butterflies

I wonder if they are blue,
Or orange and brown,
I wonder if I can hear the flutter of the wings,
If I do not make any sound,
I wonder if they may land on my shoulder,
As I hold in my breath,
I wonder if they might fly of,
Or flutter away, if I don't do my best.
My hope is that they stay,
My hope is that they carry my words
Into the deepest parts of your mind,
Reminders of memories,
Ones left behind.
I wonder if they may stay,
And they fill up the room,
And really I guess,
I don't mind at all if they do,
Because truth be told,
I wrote this for you.

For Gill McKay

Mum

It was halfway down the stairs,
And Stevie Nicks,
It was going to London,
With only a twix,
No big plans just adventures ahead,
It was always ok, with you.

It was treasure hunts,
And nanny's for lunch,
It was Paris on the ferry,
And Christmas was merry.

It was brand new shoes,
It was debating the news,
It was flying with wings,
And studying kings

It was having the most and having the least,
It was always enough,
It was both beauty and beast

It was a feeling of home,
It was never alone,
It was holding the fort,
It was just as you taught

It was phone calls all day,
But never enough,
It was being best friends,
No matter what.

It was messy and brilliant,
Some vital life lessons,
It was being your daughter,
It was everything.

Depth

Depth is something that can't be seen,
Much like pain, or love, or even fear.
Depth is only known by the holder of it,
Only felt by the mere few close to it,
But held in the hearts of all humans.
Sometimes, as we travel along in this busy life,
We forget to hold space for others strife,
We forget to hold space for depth.
We see the surface, the glide, the glimmer of a
smile, or the flicker of a glance,
But we don't see the depth,
We don't hold space for it.
We judge quickly,
We berate loudly,
And we tolerate little.
We have forgotten the depth of the human soul,
We have forgotten to hold space,
To offer discernment,
To be gentle with each other,
Life is busy I know,
Often we have much to do,
and places to go,
But just for today,
Just in this hour,
See past the surface, the glide, the glimmer of a
smile or the glance,
And look for the depth of the soul,
And you shall see the most wonderful dance.
As when we do this, for others,
and ourselves too,

You'll truly see me,
and I'll truly see you.

UP

I'm going up In the world,
Not in your world, just mine.
I decided ups the right way.
Choosing up, come what may.
Within the frown you travel down,
And if not careful,
You can drown,
So I'm going up,
And filling my cup,
And choosing to live just a little bit taller,
Shoulders back,
Lungs open wide,
Speaking my truth,
Authentic with pride

Don't make waves that you can't ride,
Don't trust people, not on your side,
I can swim, so I think I'll be fine,
And if I don't at least try,
I never will shine.

Open Mic

I might do something brave,
I might pretend the nerves are excitement, you
know, like Mel Robbins said.
I might pretend that standing on stage,
Holding the mic,
Doesn't fill me with dread.
I might just do it, fuck it,
After all,
We're a long time dead.
I might just not try to hard,
Or overthink it,
Or worry what might,
And I might just let the words flow and be and live
and love and breath.
I might just speak,
It's not something I can't do,
It's just become something I won't do,
A big brick wall of fear,
I guess it's built with words like
Failure, stupid, to quiet, too loud,
Too scruffy, too something, but nothing that makes
me proud.
Perhaps if I did it, and just didn't worry,
And slow down my words, remember no hurry,
Perhaps, perhaps, perhaps,
It will all just work out fine,
People might even clap,
Enjoying my spoken words,
Feeling the little arm hairs rise,
As something stirs, something inside.

It might even be magic,
It might be nothing at all,
But one thing is for certain,
To live in fear,
To fear the unknown,
To never show yourself, how much you've grown,
Well what then?

The Comparison Thief

That could be you you know,
Yeah I know that seems far fetched,
So much further or father ahead,
Is that the same word, I'm really not sure -
I'll check it out, come on in, close the door.
Your just good enough, I know you don't think it
but really it's true,
Just good enough, and enough and that's you. And
yeah they seem better,
But better than what?
That's comparison my friend,
Of something you're not.
So anyway listen,
You're doing just fine,
Walking your path whilst I'm walking mine,
And people might poke, or laugh and make fun,
But you will be laughing when this is all done,
Cos you stepped out, and you got a bit brave, you
didn't just sit there, quiet and safe. And that's
pretty cool to be fair, don't you think? You didn't
just follow, or make yourself shrink.
I think that's cool,
And I think you're enough,
So come on now,
We can sail the rough.

'Maybe tomorrow she whispered, and then she did it anyway'

Mabon

I've lost my spark again,
I hope that it comes back,
The thoughts are swirling round,
Reminding everything I lack

I lost it in the day to day
Life just whizzing past,
They tell you all the time,
It's true, it goes so very fast

I lost it in the piles of washing,
I lost it in the dirty sink,
I lost it in the unswept floor,
So much to do, no time to think

It's Mabon tomorrow,
And it's come with perfect time,
A gentle nudge, a soft reminder,
It always works out fine

The autumn equinox,
The thanks for what's been grown,
The gentle steps of Persephone,
As she travels home

Perhaps the sparks not gone,
Perhaps it is just faded,
Just like the sun,
I've shone all year,
And now it's time to rest

Let's decorate the house,
With little dried out orange stars,
Let's pull the blankets up,
And rest our weary feet,
You've done enough my sweet

The harvest has been bountiful,
Apples and berries of growth,
Your kindness has shone through,
You've done all that you could do.

Perhaps the sparks not gone,
Perhaps it's just Mabon.
Time to go within,
To think of all that you have done,
And battles that you've won.

Happy Autumn Equinox,
Happy Mabon.

Autumn

Its the blanket pulled over just one leg,
The lit fire, but not for long,
Its the smell of the new pumpkin spice candle,
But only 2 nights this week.
It's a Netflix binge, and sofa days,
It's big long walks and crunchy leaves,
It's dewy damp air, and sprinkles of cold,
It's the sun still warming our cheeks,
And the slow cooker dusted of, stew for weeks!
It's not quite finished, but beautifully calm, like
mixing the paints and creating the most beautiful
colours.
It's bubbly baths and popcorn bowls,
Its uniforms washed, but not on the line,
Or maybe it will dry, but not quite in time.
It's letting it go, and learning to be,
Still up early, but taking things slow,
Places to be but nowhere to go
It's Fleetwood Mac and football Saturdays, its cafe
coffee with fellow
Mums.
It's yellow, orange and red.
It's leaving harsh words, left unsaid.
It's gentle, it's slow, and letting it go.
The season is autumn,
The grass needs a mow!

The Formula for Success

I heard someone say that the formula for success is to double your rate of failure. Imagine if failure wasn't a word with such weight, it sounds all grey and heavy.
Like a big rock that won't move.
Imagine if we made it light and fluffy, like a cloud, using it to bounce onto the next, until the golden sunshine of success is reached. Each cloud soaked in learning and wisdom. And remember it's fluffy, and bouncy, and it does not hurt to fall onto the word of failure. It does not hurt because it means that you tried, and you know you'll try again, maybe not today, but maybe tomorrow, and maybe that time will be the time. Isn't it wonderful to try, to bounce amongst the fluffy clouds of failure whilst we find our way, find our wings, find success and all that that in tails.
The clouds of failure are a beautiful place to be, it's the place of attempts, the place of lessons, the place of being vulnerable and honest and true. The place that we soak up the wisdom. And perhaps sometimes, we release through the clouds some tears, that's ok, the grass always needs a little rain, it's helping you grow, and really you know, that it's always the way, and on you go.
I'd much rather bounce of the fluffy clouds of failure than to sit in stagnant pools of comfort, and although I've never been very good at maths, I think the sunshine of success will always be reached if we apply this formula, don't you?

So keep trying cloud surfer, you'll get there. I'll give you a wave as our clouds float by one another.

Thank you for meeting me here, in these pages, between the pauses, in the space where healing lives.

*If my words found you,
I hope they reminded you that you're never alone in becoming.*

Keep growing. Keep choosing yourself. Keep becoming everything you were always meant to be.

With Love

Harriet

Acknowledgements

I am so very grateful to friends, family, my amazing parents, my wonderful husband Sam, who reminded me again and again that I am enough. Thank you to all the women in Women Who Don't Drink for believing in this book before I did, especially Steph. Without all of you, this book would never exist, and I would still be stuck on the hamster wheel. Also to Aaron and Connie, remember your name, you can do anything and be anyone. This world is limitless, as are you.

About the Author

Harriet writes to make sense of moments that are fleeting, uncertain and unfinished. 'Maybe Tomorrow' is her first collection of poems written during times of the challenges faced when removing alcohol. An exploration of time, joy, doubt, and the slow work of becoming. When not writing, she can be found with her family and dogs, collecting notebooks and drinking way to much coffee. Harriet runs the 'Women's Wellness Group' in Upton Upon Severn, supporting women to remove, reduce or take a break from alcohol and volunteers as a group expert and peer mentor for Women Who Don't Drink. Harriet is training to become an ICF accredited coach whilst running her family business, a petrol station in Upton Upon Severn. Harriet believes poems are small reminders that we are always in motion, always changing.

Useful Resources

If you or someone you love is navigating their relationship with alcohol and is looking for support, these organisations can help.

www.womenwhodontdrink.com

www.nacoa.org.uk

www.wearewithyou.org.uk

www.smartrecovery.org.uk

www.mind.org.uk

www.samaritans.org

www.cranstoun.org

giveusashout.org

www.alcoholics-anonymous.org.uk

al-anonuk.org.uk

Connect with Me

For more poetry, guidance and alcohol free inspiration-

Instagram : @harrietelstonpoetry

@harrietelstoncoaching

Facebook : Harriet Elston

The Women's Wellness Group

TikTok : @harrietelstonpoetry

Website : www.harrietelstoncoaching.co.uk

Printed in Dunstable, United Kingdom